TOP 10
SPORTS
★STARS★

BASKETBALL'S
TOP 10

SCORERS

Barry Wilner

Enslow Publishers, Inc.
40 Industrial Road
Box 398
Berkeley Heights, NJ 07922
USA

http://www.enslow.com

Library of Congress Cataloging-in-Publication Data

Wilner, Barry.
  Basketball's top 10 scorers / Barry Wilner.
      p. cm. — (Top 10 sports stars)
  Includes bibliographical references and index.
  Summary: "A collective biography of the top 10 basketball scorers, both
past and present, which includes accounts of game action, career statistics,
and more"—Provided by publisher.
  ISBN 978-0-7660-3470-9
  1. Basketball players—Statistics—Juvenile literature. 2. Basketball—
Records—Juvenile literature. I. Title.
  GV885.1.W55 2011
  796.323'640922—dc22

  [B]

                                    2009036708

Printed in the United States of America

052010 Lake Book Manufacturing, Inc., Melrose Park, IL

10 9 8 7 6 5 4 3 2 1

To Our Readers: We have done our best to make sure all Internet
Addresses in this book were active and appropriate when we went to
press. However, the author and the publisher have no control over and
assume no liability for the material available on those Internet sites or on
other Web sites they may link to. Any comments or suggestions can be sent
by e-mail to comments@enslow.com or to the address on the back cover.

♻ Enslow Publishers, Inc., is committed to printing our books on recycled
paper. The paper in every book contains 10% to 30% post-consumer waste
(PCW). The cover board on the outside of each book contains 100% PCW.
Our goal is to do our part to help young people and the environment too!

Illustration Credits: All photos courtesy of Associated Press, except pp. 38
and 42, courtesy NBAE/Getty Images.

Cover Illustration: Associated Press.

TOP 10

CONTENTS

Dunks and long three-pointers. Spinning layups and graceful hook shots. Even free throws.

The points just piled up for the top scorers in the National Basketball Association (NBA), whether they were leading fast breaks or jamming home passes. Some stood near the basket, waiting to be fed the ball for a monstrous, rim-rocking throwdown. Others used lightning-quick first steps to drive down the lane, float through the air, and softly lay in the ball.

All were great. All were winners because, after all, the idea of the game is to score points.

Nobody did that better than Kareem Abdul-Jabbar, a six-time NBA MVP whose 38,387 points are the most in pro basketball history. He invented the "Sky Hook"—an unblockable shot that became like a lay-in for the 7-foot-2 center who also dominated college basketball when his name was Lew Alcindor.

Another brilliant center was the powerful Wilt Chamberlain, the only man to score 100 points in an NBA game. Chamberlain could palm the ball as if it were an egg, yet his gentle finger rolls made it seem as if the ball could break as he gently laid it in the basket.

For sheer grace, it has been the shooting guards who seemed to fly who truly made the NBA so popular. Michael Jordan, the MVP of all six NBA Finals in which he played—and won—is considered by many the best player ever. Kobe Bryant, the nearest thing to Jordan, has become an unstoppable force with the ball. Reggie Miller was the most dangerous shooter from downtown the league has seen. And Jerry West, so pure a shooter and memorable a player that his silhouette serves as the NBA logo, also was a pinpoint passer and excellent defender.

Not that guards are the only ones who can pile up the points. Three forwards always mentioned among the top scorers are Larry Bird, Karl Malone, and Elvin Hayes.

Bird was a deadly outside shooter from anywhere on the court, and he was so confident in his skills he challenged defenders to come try to stop him. They couldn't.

Malone was the perfect power forward, a man whose strength let him dominate under the boards. Hayes, the Big E, never took a shot he thought would miss. He rarely did.

And then there was the Big O, Oscar Robertson, who once averaged a triple-double for a season. Everything that the other great scorers specialized in, Robertson also could do.

Put these ten men on the court against each other and each side might score a thousand points.
Or more.

KAREEM ABDUL-JABBAR

KAREEM
ABDUL-JABBAR

In the entire history of the NBA, no one has scored more points or won more Most Valuable Player awards than Kareem Abdul-Jabbar.

The 7-foot-2 center who won three straight NCAA championships with UCLA before becoming the top overall draft pick in 1969, went on to capture his first pro title in his second season with the Milwaukee Bucks. After being traded to Los Angeles in 1975, he led the Lakers to five more NBA crowns.

Those six titles matched his six MVP honors, and when Abdul-Jabbar put in his last sky hook—that unblockable sweeping soft shot that became his trademark—he had concluded his Hall of Fame career with 38,387 points, more than 1,000 beyond anyone else.

"There's a ball. There's a hoop. You put the ball through the hoop," Abdul-Jabbar once joked.[1]

Abdul-Jabbar developed from a rail-thin high school star named Lew Alcindor to a strong, graceful, and dominant performer. He changed his name for religious reasons while he was with the Bucks, but he never changed his game.

Abdul-Jabbar would set up just outside the lane, many times with two players guarding him once he got the ball. Because he was an excellent passer, he often would find teammates for open shots. More often, though, he would shoot. And hit.

Beginning with his Rookie of the Year campaign for Milwaukee, when Abdul-Jabbar scored 28.8 points a game, he averaged at least 21 a game in each of the first seventeen seasons of his twenty-year career, leading the league in scoring twice. He made the All-Star Game in all but one of his seasons and twice was MVP of the finals. The numbers were just as special in the playoffs—a 24.3 average.

"Why judge anymore?" asked Pat Riley, who coached Abdul-Jabbar during the Lakers' "Showtime" days. "When a man has broken records, won championships, endured tremendous criticism and responsibility, why judge? Let's toast him as the greatest player ever."[2]

He was certainly the greatest scorer ever. And it was not only with backboard-shaking dunks or that famed sky hook; Abdul-Jabbar was a good foul shooter, rare among big men. Less rare among tall, athletic centers was Abdul-Jabbar's shot-blocking skills. He retired in 1989 at age forty-two with the most in league history: 3,189.

KAREEM ABDUL-JABBAR

BORN: April 16, 1947, New York, New York.

HIGH SCHOOL: Power Memorial High School, New York, New York.

COLLEGE: University of California, Los Angeles (UCLA).

PRO CAREER: Milwaukee Bucks (1969–75); Los Angeles Lakers (1975–89).

RECORDS: NBA Most Career Points (38,387); Minutes Played (57,446); Field Goals (15,837); Most NBA All-Star Games (18).

HONORS: Basketball Hall of Fame (1995); NBA Most Valuable Player (1971, 1972, 1974, 1976, 1977, 1980); NBA Finals Most Valuable Player (1971, 1985).

LARRY BIRD

LARRY
BIRD

He was supposed to be too slow and not strong enough to become a star. So Larry Bird soared powerfully through college basketball, nearly winning an NCAA title with Indiana State.

And then "Larry Legend" dominated the NBA with the Boston Celtics on his way to the Basketball Hall of Fame.

Bird brought a lot more to the game than basketball smarts and a near-perfect shooting eye from anywhere on the court. He was so confident that he'd tell opponents he was going to score 40 points, then do it. He once asked the other players in the All-Star Game's

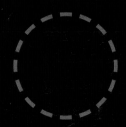

three-point shooting contest which one was going to finish second—to him. Then he won it.

"Larry is something special. I'll never forget those battles," said Magic Johnson, the Lakers' great guard and one of Bird's best friends in the NBA. "That man is one of those guys who actually scared me to death. He could beat you at any time and in so many ways. It was scary."[1]

When Bird joined the Celtics in 1979, they were struggling. The most successful team in NBA history, the Celtics had become losers. Bird quickly changed that, winning the league's Rookie of the Year honors, as Boston won 61 games, 32 better than the season before.

A year later, the Celtics were NBA champions, and Bird had averaged almost exactly the same points (21.2 per game) as in his rookie year (21.3). From there, Bird would score at least 20 points a game in nine seasons and finish with a 24.3 points average for his 12-season career.

He scored 60 points in a game against Atlanta in 1985, when he averaged 28.7 a game. Two seasons later, Bird went for 29.9 a game, a career high. His baskets came from everywhere.

But Bird was about so much more than points. He could hardly jump, but he was a strong rebounder and was able to block shots. He was the best passer of any forward the NBA has seen. And he was a great leader.

"The way he attacks a challenge, nothing he accomplishes is a surprise to me," said Chris Mullin, who played with Bird on the 1992 Olympic Dream Team that won a gold medal. "If he wanted to be an actor, I wouldn't be surprised if he won an Oscar for his first movie. He works hard to achieve success."[2]

That included three straight NBA Most Valuable Player awards (1984, 1985, and 1986) and three league championships. He made the All-NBA team nine times, was the NBA Finals MVP twice, and was voted one of the 50 greatest players in league history.

LARRY BIRD

BORN: December 7, 1956, West Baden, Indiana.

· ·

HIGH SCHOOL: Springs Valley High School, French Lick, Indiana.

· ·

COLLEGE: Indiana State University.

· ·

PRO CAREER: Boston Celtics, 1979–1992.

· ·

RECORDS: NBA 3-Point Field Goal Leader (1985–86, 1986–87); NBA Best Free Throw Percentage (1983–84, 1985–87, 1989–90).

· ·

HONORS: Basketball Hall of Fame (1998); NBA MVP (1984, '85, '86); NBA Final MVP (1984, '86); NBA All-Star Game MVP (1982); NBA Rookie of the Year (1980).

· ·

KOBE BRYANT

KOBE
BRYANT

Kobe Bryant is the best basketball scorer never to go to college. When you consider how many of the NBA's greatest players went right from high school to the pros, that's impressive.

Bryant got an early start on a career in which he has won three NBA championships, two scoring titles and one MVP award. He went from Lower Merion High in Pennsylvania to the Lakers in 1996 as an 18-year-old first-round draft pick, although the Charlotte Hornets selected him, then traded him to Los Angeles. By his second season, he was a starter in the All-Star Game.

The son of former NBA player Joe Bryant, Kobe combined with Shaquille O'Neal to win those three rings in 2000, 2001, and '02. But it wasn't until O'Neal was traded to Miami that Bryant became a dominant player and unstoppable scorer.

In fact, Jerry West, the Lakers' all-time top scorer before Kobe came along, believes Bryant could hold every points record before his career ends.

"He's a Picasso in basketball shoes, absolutely—one of those once-in-a-lifetime players," West said, comparing Bryant to a great artist. "Kobe is the ultimate closer in the game. In all sports you seem to have people who play at a high level when it's important. You don't see anyone do it like him today, you really don't."[1]

As Bryant climbed toward the top 10 in scoring, he had an incredible 81-point night against Toronto and also had games of 65, 62, and 60. Through his MVP season of 2007–08, Bryant had 24 games with at least 50 points.

The 81-pointer is second only to Wilt Chamberlain's magnificent 100-point performance in 1962. It brought a phone call from Magic Johnson that was a special moment for Bryant.

"For him to just call me and tell me what a great game it was and how proud of me he is meant more to me than the 81 points," Bryant said. "That meant more to me than even the game itself because I idolized him as a kid."[2]

Bryant has done his scoring in many different ways. He is good from three-point range and deadly from inside the arc. He's one of the best drivers in the game, which means he also often gets fouled as he goes to the basket. And he's an excellent free-throw shooter.

When the game is on the line, Bryant is as good as any of the NBA's great scorers. It doesn't matter how many defenders try to stop him, Kobe Bryant will go after his shot. And usually make it.

KOBE BRYANT

BORN: August 23, 1978, Philadelphia, Pennsylvania.

. . . .

HIGH SCHOOL: Lower Merion High School, Ardmore, Pennsylvania.

. . . .

PRO CAREER: Los Angeles Lakers, 1996–present.

. . . .

RECORDS: Most Points by a Guard in a Game (81); Youngest Player to Score 18,000 Points (28 years, 156 days).

. . . .

HONORS: NBA Most Valuable Player (2008); NBA Finals Most Valuable Player (2009); NBA All-Star Game Most Valuable Player (2007).

. . . .

WILT CHAMBERLAIN

WILT
CHAMBERLAIN

Imagine scoring 100 points in a pro basketball game. Only one NBA player ever did it: Wilt Chamberlain.

Oddly, Chamberlain got the 100 in Hershey, Pennsylvania, in a non-televised game and with almost no national media covering the contest. When news spread that "Wilt the Stilt" hit the century mark for the Philadelphia Warriors against the New York Knicks, there was disbelief among fans, but not among players.

"We were talking about Wilt, how he was going to score 100 points in a game real soon," Lakers superstar Jerry West said of a plane ride the team took on March 2, 1962. "When we got off the airplane, somebody said, 'Hey, did you hear about Wilt Chamberlain? He scored 100 points in a game.' That's one record that will never be broken, I can assure you."[1]

So far, West is right. Nobody has come close to the Big Dipper's mark.

Chamberlain, who stood 7-foot-1 and weighed more than 300 pounds, dominated around and underneath the basket. As he filled out from a skinny high school center in Philadelphia to an All-American at Kansas, opponents began to wilt when facing Wilt. After a short time with the Harlem Globetrotters, Chamberlain joined the Warriors and became NBA Rookie of the Year, scoring 37.6 points a game.

From that great start, Chamberlain got even better. He led the league in scoring in each of his first seven seasons— only Michael Jordan has matched the seven straight—and averaged an unimaginable 50.4 points a game in 1961–62. For his 14-year career, Wilt wound up with a 30.1 average. Fifteen times, he scored at least 65 points in a game and 118 times Chamberlain had at least 50.

He did most of his scoring with thunderous dunks. Chamberlain also used a finger-roll from the level of the basket—or even above—and a fadeaway shot that was unblockable.

"Wilt was one of the greatest ever, and we will never see another one like him," said Kareem Abdul-Jabbar, who broke Chamberlain's career scoring record in 1984.[2]

A four-time NBA Most Valuable Player (1960, 1966–1968), Wilt also was a brilliant rebounder, passer, and shot-blocker. He holds the record for rebounds in a game (55) and assists by a center (702 in 1967–68).

Overall, Chamberlain won two NBA titles, one with the Philadelphia 76ers in 1967 and one with the Los Angeles Lakers in 1972.

WILT CHAMBERLAIN

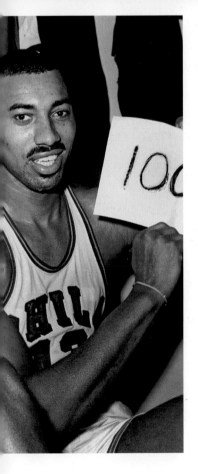

BORN: August 21, 1936, Philadelphia, Pennsylvania.

DIED: October 12, 1999, Bel Air, California.

HIGH SCHOOL: Overbrook High School, PA

COLLEGE: University of Kansas.

PRO CAREER: Philadelphia/San Francisco Warriors, 1959–65; Philadelphia 76ers, 1965–68; Los Angeles Lakers, 1968–73.

RECORDS: Many, including most points in a game (100) and career rebounds (23,924).

HONORS: Basketball Hall of Fame (1979); NBA Most Valuable Player (1960, '66, '67, '68); NBA Finals MVP (1972).

ELVIN HAYES

ELVIN
HAYES

Little did Elvin Hayes know that when he was detoured from detention in the eighth grade and taken instead to the school gym, he was beginning a Hall-of-Fame basketball career.

At 6-foot-9, Hayes became one of the NBA's great big men, perhaps the best outside shooter for his position ever.

Before starring with three pro teams for sixteen seasons, making twelve All-Star Games and winning the NBA championship in 1977–78 with the Washington Bullets, Hayes was an All-American at the University of Houston. In 1968, he averaged 36.8 points a game, was voted player of the year, and led the Cougars to victory over UCLA in college basketball's "Game of the Century," scoring 39 points and grabbing 15 rebounds. That was the first nationally televised college basketball game, played before a crowd of 52,693, until then the largest attendance at a basketball game. And Hayes was at his best that night, outplaying the great Kareem Abdul-Jabbar.

"No one ever dreamed it would be the biggest game in the history of basketball," Hayes said. "No one thought of that before the game. We left the locker room saying, 'We hope someone's there at the game.'

"It changed my life, no question about it. Afterward, everyone knew Elvin Hayes."[1]

Pretty good stuff for someone who used to say prayers as a teenager that he would someday succeed in the sport.

"It's a long road," added Hayes, whose 27,313 points ranked him third in NBA scoring when he retired in 1984. "To see a kid's dream and then be able to touch that dream and have it become reality."[2]

Hayes not only was a pinpoint shooter from long range in a day when big men rarely moved so far away from the basket, he was a terrific rebounder. That made him even more dangerous, because opposing forwards had to be quick enough to guard him on the outside and powerful enough to stop him underneath the basket. They hardly ever were.

Hayes averaged 21 points and 12.5 rebounds a game

for his career. In 1973–74, he pulled down nearly as many rebounds (18.1) as he scored points (21.4) per game.

"I really don't believe I did those things . . . that I could have scored all those points and got those rebounds," he said. "My greatest fear every year I played was that I would be cut and wouldn't make the team."[3]

ELVIN HAYES

BORN: November 17, 1945, Rayville, Louisiana.

HIGH SCHOOL: Eula D. Britton, Rayville, Loisiana.

COLLEGE: University of Houston.

PRO CAREER: San Diego/Houston Rockets, 1968–72; Baltimore/Washington Bullets, 1972–81; Houston Rockets, 1981–84.

RECORDS: Fifth in NBA Games Played (1,303) and Third in Minutes Played (50,000); missed only nine games in sixteen years.

HONORS: Basketball Hall of Fame (1990); NBA Draft First Overall Pick (1968); twelve-time NBA All-Star.

MICHAEL JORDAN

MICHAEL
JORDAN

MJ. His Airness. Or just plain Michael.

Michael Jordan reached that special position in life that he was as well known by his nicknames, or merely by his first name, as anything else.

Jordan climbed so high by being able to fly so high over the basketball court. Watching MJ soar through the air for his memorable dunks, it sure looked like gravity had no hold on the man.

"Is MJ the greatest player scorer ever? Next question," said Charles Barkley, one of Jordan's strongest competitors and closest friends during their Hall of Fame careers. "He's the greatest PLAYER ever."[1]

Jordan led the Chicago Bulls to six NBA championships in eight seasons, and he didn't play for most of the two years the Bulls fell short. After a third straight title in 1993, Jordan left basketball to try his hand at baseball, where he struggled in the minor leagues before returning to the Bulls late in the 1994–95 schedule. In '96, '97 and '98, he again carried the Bulls to championships.

And while Air Jordan always will be praised for his flights to the basket, his most memorable shot remains the jumper that beat the Utah Jazz for the sixth and final title. MJ even held his pose, his long arm extended in perfect shooting form as the winning shot went down.

"I was getting tired and I guess the lessons that you learn over the years is stick with that shot a little longer, make sure you get that extra little bit," Jordan said. "And that was my thinking, was to make sure that I extend and do the necessary fundamentals to get the ball to the basket.

"It turned out to look as if I was posing for all the photographers, but that was not the case."[2]

Then he retired again, although Jordan made an aborted comeback with the Washington Wizards, joining them as team president but eventually returning to the court.

A five-time Most Valuable Player, Jordan made the All-NBA squad 10 times. He was the 1985 Rookie of the Year, the 1988 Defensive Player of the Year—yes, this great scorer was a top defender, too—and a double Olympic gold medalist. In 1996, he was selected one of the 50 greatest players in NBA history.

But as Barkley mentioned, most people consider MJ to be No. 1. And it's hard to dispute considering all those brilliant numbers. From his college days, when he knocked down the winning jump shot for North Carolina in the 1982 NCAA championship game, through his fifteen seasons in the NBA, Jordan was unstoppable. His career average was 30.1 points in the regular season, 33.4 in the playoffs.

MICHAEL JORDAN

BORN: February 17, 1963, Brooklyn, N.Y.

HIGH SCHOOL: Emsley A. Laney High School, Wilmington, North Carolina.

COLLEGE: University of North Carolina.

PRO CAREER: Chicago Bulls, 1985–93, 1995–98; Washington Wizards, 2001–03.

RECORDS: NBA Most Career Playoff Points (5,987); NBA Most Playoff Points in a Game (63); NBA Points Per Game Average (31.5).

HONORS: Basketball Hall of Fame (2009); NBA Most Valuable Player (1988, '92, '92, '96, '98); NBA Finals Most Valuable Player (1991, '92, '93, '96, '97, '98).

KARL MALONE

KARL
MALONE

The basketball term "power forward" wasn't invented for Karl Malone. He simply fit that description—and that position—the best of anyone in NBA history.

At 6-foot-9 and 255 pounds, Malone was powerful. He also was quick, smart and dependable, which explains his nickname: "The Mailman."

Throughout his nineteen-year pro career, Malone was one of the NBA's biggest stars. He won the league's Most Valuable Player Award twice (1997 and 1999), was voted to the All-NBA team 11 times and twice was the All-Star Game's MVP, won Olympic gold medals in

1992 and 1996 for the United States, and in '96 was selected as one of the 50 greatest players in league history. Karl Malone delivered. And when he was done, he trailed only Kareem Abdul-Jabbar in all-time scoring, with 36,928 points.

"Those numbers are way out there and if just a few things changed, he could have put them out there even further," said Jazz star guard John Stockton, Malone's long-time teammate.[1]

Eighteen of those seasons were spent with Stockton on the Utah Jazz, who drafted Malone in the first round, 13th overall, in 1985 out of Louisiana Tech, hardly a basketball powerhouse. But the Jazz saw something special in Malone, and he rewarded them by averaging more than 20 points in seventeen seasons.

Together, Malone and Stockton perfected the pick-and-roll play. The strong Malone would stand near the top of the key, from 15 to 20 feet from the basket. Stockton, the NBA's career assist leader, handled the ball as Malone stood to block Stockton's defender. Malone would then roll toward the basket, and Stockton would either shoot if his defender was out of position or, more often, pass to Malone for a layup or a thunderous dunk.

That play, run thousands of times by Malone and Stockton, now is represented by statues of the two players outside the Salt Lake City arena where they made their fame.

"It all worked because of the big fella in the middle," Stockton said.[2]

Malone's No. 32 jersey was retired by the Jazz in 2006 and hangs in the arena's rafters. It is a reminder of the rugged defense, powerful rebounding, and offensive brilliance he brought to the court.

When you mention a mailman, you don't normally think about a superstar. When you mention the NBA's Mailman, you think about one of the sport's greatest scorers.

KARL MALONE

BORN: July 24, 1963, Summerfield, Louisiana.

HIGH SCHOOL: Summerfield High School, Summerfield, Louisiana.

COLLEGE: Louisiana Tech.

PRO CAREER: Utah Jazz, 1985–2003; Los Angeles Lakers, 2003–04.

RECORDS: Second in NBA Career Points (36,928); Most Career Free Throws Attempted (13,188); Most Career Defensive Rebounds (11,406).

HONORS: NBA Most Valuable Player (1997, 1999); NBA All-Star Game Most Valuable Player (1989, 1993).

REGGGIE MILLER

REGGIE
MILLER

Some fans believe pro basketball's three-point shot was invented for Reggie Miller. Not quite, although no player was ever better from long-range.

As an All-American at UCLA, Miller was a great shooter, but some questioned how well he would adapt to the NBA's more physical game. Drafted 11th by the Indiana Pacers, even though many fans wanted them to take local college hero Steve Alford, Miller instead found a home in Indianapolis for 19 seasons.

He was most at home firing away from the outside. As a rookie, Miller broke Larry

Bird's record for most three-pointers by a first-year player. And he never looked back.

"I think he has the capability of becoming a very good NBA player and I think he's had a good season," Pacers coach Jack Ramsay said after the 1987–88 season. "Overall he's made good progress at both ends of the court."[1]

That progress never stopped. By his third season, Miller was among the NBA's top sharpshooters, averaging a career-high 24.6 points a game. He remained there for a decade, with his skills at driving to the basket and getting to the free-throw line making him one of the most well-rounded scorers of his day.

Although he never won an NBA title, Miller played in some of the most memorable games ever. His battles with the Knicks at Madison Square Garden in New York became legendary.

In the 1994 playoffs, Reggie had a running conversation with movie director Spike Lee sitting courtside in his Knicks jersey, even while Miller was scoring 25 of his 39 points in the fourth quarter. Indiana went on to win the game, 93–86.

"Spike and I were just having some fun," Miller said with a laugh. "I wasn't having a very good game and he was kind of ribbing me. After I hit that first 3, I kind of looked at him and started talking to him and after that, it was history."[2]

Not quite. The next year Miller was at it again. In an amazing 8.9 seconds at the end of Game 1 of the Eastern Conference semifinals, Reggie scored eight points on two three-pointers, a steal, a rebound, and two free throws in a 107–105 win.

"I've had some of my better moments against this team in this building," Miller said after his final game in the Garden, when he received a huge ovation. "A lot of things have been said both ways—me to them and them to me. I really felt the respect and the love from the New Yorkers."[3]

REGGIE MILLER

BORN: August 24, 1965, Riverside, California.

· ·

HIGH SCHOOL: Riverside Polytech, Riverside, California.

· ·

COLLEGE: University of California, Los Angeles (UCLA).

· ·

PRO CAREER: Indiana Pacers, 1987–2005.

· ·

RECORDS: NBA Best Free Throw Percentage (1990–91, 1998–99, 2000–01, 2001–02, 2004–05); Most Career 3-Point Field Goals (6,486).

· ·

HONORS: Five-time NBA All-Star.

· ·

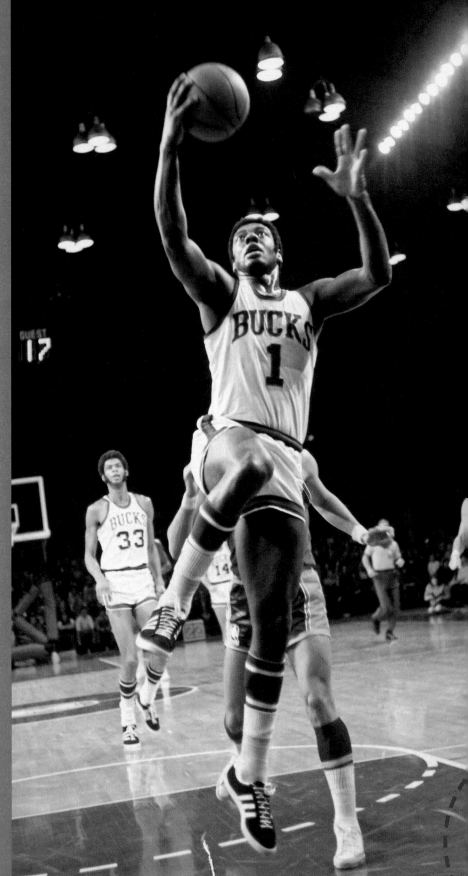

OSCAR ROBERTSON

OSCAR
ROBERTSON

Although he retired before many of today's basketball fans were born, Oscar Robertson still is considered the greatest all-around player the NBA has seen.

The "Big O" was a big-time scorer, of course, but he also was such a great ballhandler and passer, and such a strong rebounder and defender, that he practically invented the term "triple-double." In fact, Robertson averaged double digits in points, rebounds, and assists for an entire season, in his second NBA season of 1961–62. He scored 30.8 points per game, with 12.5 rebounds and 11.4 assists a night.

When Robertson left the NBA in 1974, he was the career-scoring leader among guards with 26,710 points and also was the assists leader. He's been passed in those areas since, but not by the same person.

"He is so great, he scares me," Hall of Fame coach Red Auerbach once said of Robertson.[1]

While Robertson wasn't as sharp a shooter as Jerry West—his teammate on the 1960 Olympic gold medal team—he was close. He also was 6-5, 205 pounds of muscle, which helped the "Big O" play big under the basket. Many of his points came on drives to the hoop, where he could use his size and power, or off rebounds because he was so comfortable under the basket.

"I always felt it was important to get to the basket when someone else shot," he said. "If you could keep the ball alive or score off a rebound, you helped your team as much as if you shot from the outside."[2]

The league and All-Star Game most valuable player in the 1963–64 season, Robertson played for the Cincinnati Royals during his first ten pro seasons. He made the NBA All-Star team in nine of those years after capturing Rookie of the Year honors by scoring 30.5 points and getting 10.1 rebounds and 9.7 assists a game—incredible numbers for a veteran, let alone a first-year player.

But something was missing for Oscar: a championship. The Royals, while a very good team, never could get past the Boston dynasty or some strong Philadelphia clubs.

In 1970, seeking that title, Robertson joined the Bucks in a trade. Milwaukee already had a young center, Kareem

Abdul-Jabbar—then named Lew Alcindor—and needed some veteran leadership. And some extra scoring.

Robertson provided both, averaging 19.4 points while guiding the youthful Bucks to 66 wins, the NBA's best record. He added 18.3 points a game in the playoffs and, at last, earned that championship ring.

OSCAR ROBERTSON

BORN: November 24, 1938, Charlotte, Tennessee.

. . . .

HIGH SCHOOL: Crispus Attucks High School, Indianapolis, Indiana.

. . . .

COLLEGE: University of Cincinnati.

. . . .

PRO CAREER: Cincinnati Royals, 1960–70; Milwaukee Bucks, 1970–74.

. . . .

RECORDS: NBA Assists Leader (1960–61, 1961–62, 1963–64, 1964–65, 1965–66, 1968–69); Averaged Triple-Double in 1961–62 (30.8 points, 12.5 rebounds, 11.4 assists).

. . . .

HONORS: Basketball Hall of Fame (1980); NBA MVP (1964); NBA All-Star Game MVP (1961, '64, '69); NBA Rookie of the Year (1961).

. . . .

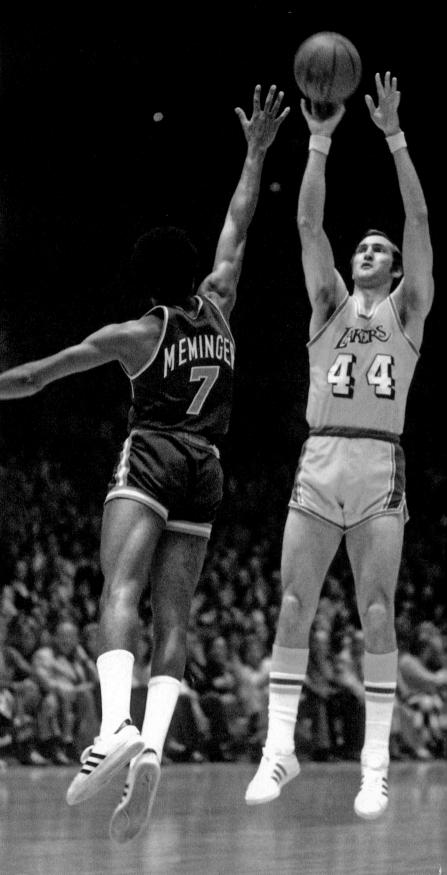

JERRY WEST

JERRY
WEST

Take a look at the official NBA logo.

That figure dribbling the basketball is none

other than Jerry West.

Known as "Mr. Clutch" for his sharp shooting from outside and "Zeke from Cabin Creek" for the town near where West was born in West Virginia, West was such a classic player that the league decided to make his silhouette its own image. And why not? There's never been a better all-around guard in the sport than West: smooth shooter, shut-down defender, great passer, and steady leader.

West played his entire career for the Los Angeles Lakers. Team owner Jerry Buss once said, "Nobody has meant more to the Los Angeles Lakers franchise than Jerry West."[1]

Who could argue? West scored 25,192 points during fourteen seasons with the team, placing him second on the franchise's all-time scoring list. (Only Kobe Bryant has scored more points playing for the Lakers.) He made the All-Star game every season of his career, averaged 27 points per game, and won the 1972 NBA title. In 1980, West entered the Hall of Fame. Sixteen years later, he was selected one of the 50 greatest players in NBA history.

West also was a key player for the 1960 U.S. Olympic team that won a gold medal. That squad, along with the 1992 Dream Team, is considered the best ever put together and had four Hall of Famers on it.

An All-American at West Virginia University, where a street was renamed Jerry West Blvd. in 2000, West led the Mountaineers to the national championship game, where they lost to California. After the Olympics, he joined the Lakers—and never looked back.

The release on his jump shot was so quick that even the NBA's best defenders couldn't come close to blocking it. West was at his best shooting off the dribble, and his perfect release for years was used as a teaching tool by coaches: "Shoot like this, shoot like Jerry West."

To West, any shot that missed didn't make sense.

"I'm surprised when the ball doesn't go into the hoop," West said. "I think I should make every shot."[2]

He made enough of them—and enough free throws, where he was a lifetime 81 percent shooter—to average more than 30 points a game four times and more than 25 points a game in eleven of his fourteen pro seasons.

JERRY WEST

BORN: May 28, 1938, Chelyan, West Virginia.

. . . .

HIGH SCHOOL: East Bank High School, East Bank, West Virginia.

. . . .

COLLEGE: West Virginia.

. . . .

PRO CAREER: Los Angeles Lakers, 1960–74.

. . . .

RECORDS: Playoff Career Points and Series Scoring Average (at retirement); fourteen-time NBA All-Star.

. . . .

HONORS: Basketball Hall of Fame (1980); NBA Finals Most Valuable Player (1969); NBA All-Star Most Valuable Player (1972).

. . . .

CHAPTER NOTES

CHAPTER 1. KAREEM ABDUL-JABBAR

1. The Associated Press, June 15, 2007.
2. *NBA.com: Kareem Abdul Jabbar Bio*, n.d., <http://www.nba.com/ history/players/abduljabbar_bio.html> (November 16, 2009).

CHAPTER 2. LARRY BIRD

1. Author interview, October 7, 1998.
2. The Associated Press, January 26, 1998.

CHAPTER 3. KOBE BRYANT

1. The Associated Press, June 3, 2008.
2. Darren Misener, "I Love the 80s—Kobe Makes History," *The Official Site of the Los Angeles Lakers*, January 22, 2006, <http://www.nba .com/lakers/news/kobe_history_060123.html> (November 4, 2009).

CHAPTER 4. WILT CHAMBERLAIN

1. The Associated Press, October 12, 1999.
2. Ibid.
3. Jim Heffernan, "Chamberlain Makes the 'Impossible' Possible—100 Points," *The Sporting News*, March 14, 1962, < http://www .sportingnews.com/archives/wilt/article8.html> (November 16, 2009).

CHAPTER 5. ELVIN HAYES

1. The Associated Press, December 19, 1993.
2. Pro Basketball Hall of Fame, May 16, 1990.
3. Ibid.

CHAPTER 6. MICHAEL JORDAN

1. Author interview, November 4, 2006.
2. The Associated Press, January 13, 1999.

CHAPTER 7. KARL MALONE

1. The Associated Press, March 23, 2006.
2. Ibid.

Chapter 8. REGGIE MILLER

1. Associated Press, April 12, 1988.
2. "The Big Apple's Most Hated Opponents," *New York Daily News*, June 6, 1994, <http://www.nydailynews.com/sports/galleries/the_big_apples_most_hated_opponents/> (November 4, 2009).
3. Associated Press, April 6, 2005.

Chapter 9. OSCAR ROBERTSON

1. *NBA.com: Oscar Robertson*, 2002, <http://www.nba.com/history/robertson_bio.html> (November 16, 2009).
2. Ibid.

Chapter 10. JERRY WEST

1. "Jerry West Stays in L.A.," *CNNSI.com*, September 9, 1998, <http://sportsillustrated.cnn.com/basketball/nba/news/1998/09/03/west_thursday/> (November 16, 2009).
2. *NBA.com: Jerry West Bio*, n.d., <http://www.nba.com/history/players/west_bio.html> (November 16, 2009).

FURTHER READING

Basketball Top 10. New York: DK Publishing, 2004.

Kramer, Sydelle. *Basketball's Greatest Players*. New York: Random House, 1997.

INTERNET ADDRESSES

Official NBA Site
http://www.nba.com/

The Naismith Memorial Basketball Hall of Fame
http://www.hoophall.com/